Hachette UK's policy is to use papers that are natural, renewable and recyclable products and made from wood grown in well-managed forests and other controlled sources. The logging and manufacturing processes are expected to conform to the environmental regulations of the country of origin.

To order, please visit www.hoddereducation.com or contact Customer Service at education@hachette.co.uk / +44 (0)1235 827827.

ISBN: 978 1 0360 0700 3

© Fiona Craig 2024

First published in 2024 by Hodder Education,
An Hachette UK Company
Carmelite House
50 Victoria Embankment
London EC4Y 0DZ

www.hoddereducation.com

Impression number 10 9 8 7 6 5 4 3 2 1

Year   2028 2027 2026 2025 2024

All rights reserved. Apart from any use permitted under UK copyright law, no part of this publication may be reproduced or transmitted in any form or by any means, electronic or mechanical, including photocopying and recording, or held within any information storage and retrieval system, without permission in writing from the publisher or under licence from the Copyright Licensing Agency Limited. Further details of such licences (for reprographic reproduction) may be obtained from the Copyright Licensing Agency Limited, www.cla.co.uk

Cover photo © Sergey Nivens - stock.adobe.com

Typeset by Integra Software Services Pvt. Ltd., Pondicherry, India

Printed and bound in Great Britain by Bell and Bain Ltd, Glasgow

A catalogue record for this title is available from the British Library.

Contents

Features to help you succeed ... 4

Chapter 1 Wider Context ... 5

Chapter 2 Supporting Education ... 10

Chapter 3 Safeguarding, Health and Safety and Wellbeing ... 19

Chapter 4 Behaviour ... 27

Chapter 5 Parents, Families and Carers ... 35

Chapter 6 Working with Others ... 40

Chapter 7 Child Development ... 46

Chapter 8 Observation and Assessment ... 55

Chapter 9 Reflective Practice ... 61

Chapter 10 Equality and Diversity ... 67

Chapter 11 Special Education Needs and Disability ... 76

Chapter 12 English as an Additional Language ... 87

Answers can be found online at www.hoddereducation.com/answers-and-extras

Education & Early Years T Level Exam Practice Workbook

Features to help you succeed

Each topic area starts with **recall activities** that will help you to remember important information you will need when answering exam questions. These activities include mind maps, matching exercises and filling in missing words in tables, sentences or diagrams.

Some questions include **Hints** or **Tips** next to them to give you extra advice on how to approach the question. **Hints** may suggest key points to consider when answering the question, while **Tips** explain how to answer the question, what important words included in the question mean or give guidance on common mistakes students make when answering these types of questions.

All questions will have spaces for you to write your answers.

Sample student answers are provided for some questions. These will help you understand how to gain the most marks and may ask you to think about the strengths and weaknesses of the answer and how it could be improved.

Some questions also include guidance and space to support you to **plan your answer** before you answer the question. This may identify and explain key words for you, provide tables for you to complete to help you to plan and structure your answer or include partially completed answers.

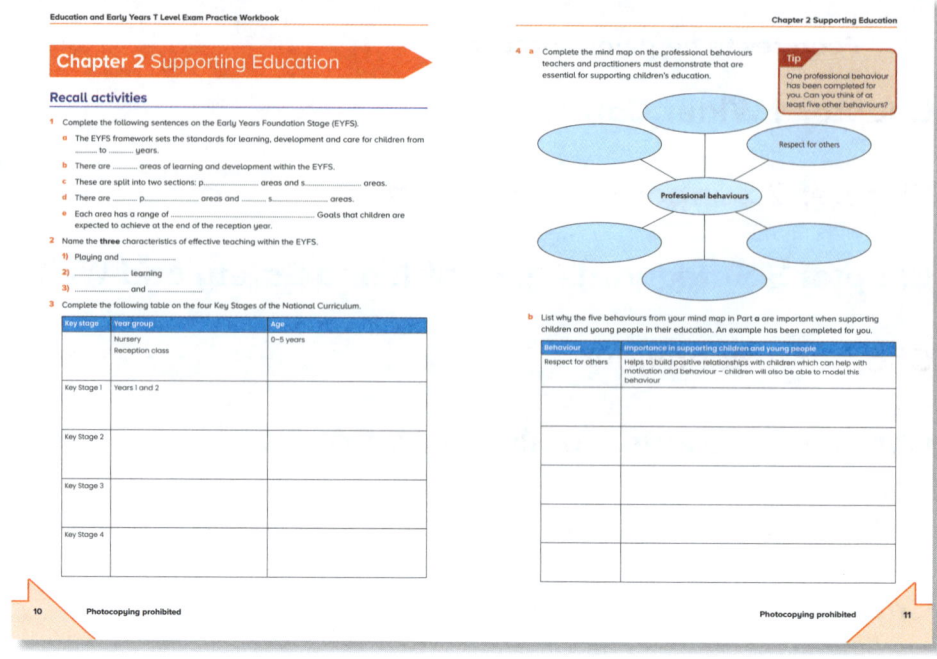

Short-answer exam practice questions help you to practice answering multiple-choice and short-answer exam questions that are typically worth 1–4 marks.

Longer-answer exam practice questions will help you to practice answering extended response questions typically worth 5–12 marks. These questions will usually include a context or scenario.

Photocopying prohibited

Chapter 1 Wider Context

Recall activities

1 Complete the mind map on the different types of provision available for children 0–5 years.

> **Hint**
> It is important that you have a good understanding of the large range of childcare and educational provision for children. Each type of provision will offer a variety of features, functions and services for children and their carers/families.

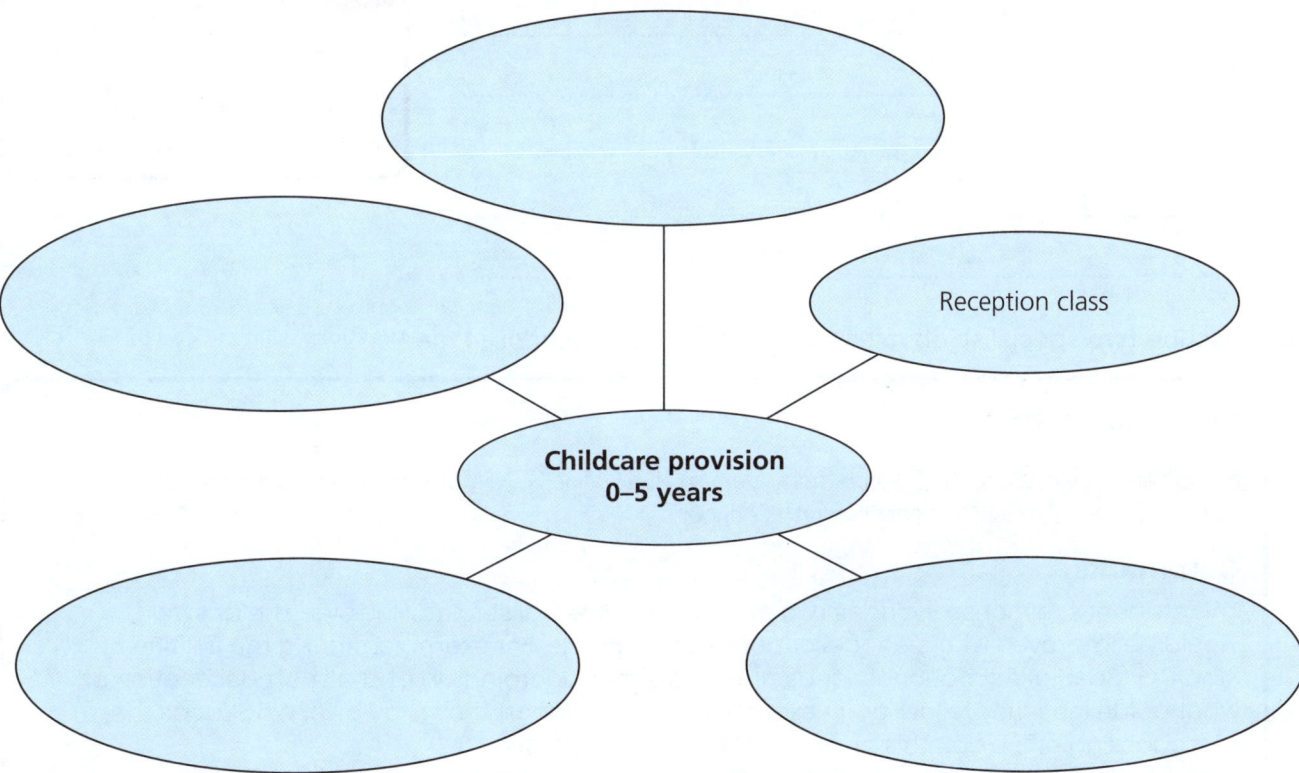

2 Draw a line to match the different types of schools with the correct definition.

School type	Definition
Academies	State-funded and no involvement from religious groups
Home schooling	These are owned by a charitable trust which is funded by the local authority
Private schooling	Educated by parents/carers at home – must have access to a full curriculum
Maintained Community schools	May work with other schools in the area (MAT) – funded through the central government
Trust schools	Paid for by fees – no government funding – also known as independent schools

Photocopying prohibited   5

Education and Early Years T Level Exam Practice Workbook

Short-answer exam-style practice questions

1 Which of the following is responsible for producing statutory guidance based on legislation for early years settings, schools and colleges. (1 mark)

   A Office for Standards in Education, Children's Services and Skills (Ofsted) ☐

   B Office for Students (OfS) ☐

   C Department for Education (DfE) ☐

   D Office of Qualifications and Examinations Regulation (Ofqual) ☐

2 Describe the roles of **two** educational professionals who would work in a primary school. (4 marks)

....

....

....

....

....

> **Tip**
>
> Questions 2 and 3 ask for **two** roles – so you must describe **two** roles to achieve full marks.

3 Describe **two** specialist job roles within a secondary school. (4 marks)

> **Sample answer**
>
> A specialist job in secondary school would be a SENDCO. The SENDCO would support the teacher. There would also be a safeguarding officer in the school.
>
> **Comments**
>
> This student's response includes two examples of specialist roles. However, the answer would be improved with clear descriptions of each role. For example, stating the full title of SENDCO (Special educational needs and disabilities coordinator) and a short description of what guidelines they follow, or an example of what support they may give. What does the safeguarding office do? This answer is likely to gain 2 marks.

Now write your own answer.

....

....

....

....

....

....

4 Identify the regulatory body that inspects and regulates childminders. (1 mark)

....

Chapter 1 Wider Context

5 Jane is a young mum of 10-month-old daughter Ruby. Jane's maternity leave is coming to an end, and she is looking for a suitable childcare setting.

   a Describe **one** type of early years provision that Jane may consider for Ruby. (2 marks)

....

....

....

....

> **Hint**
> Include type of provision, what age of children this type of setting is for and how it is funded.

   b Identify the curriculum this type of setting would follow. (1 mark)

....

Long-answer exam-style practice questions

1 Compare the similarities and differences between **two** types of provision that are available at post-16. (12 marks, plus 3 marks for QWC)

> **Tip**
> Always check your spelling and grammar as well as your answer's structure – there are 3 extra marks to gain here (and in Questions 2 and 3) for quality of written communication (QWC).

> **Plan your answer**
>
> List two types of provision and then compare what they provide. Think about:
> - What type of qualifications does the provision offer, for example, A levels?
> - Are they vocational – do they offer placement?
> - How are assessed – externally marked exams/assignments/portfolios?
> - How are they funded?
> - What are the progression routes?
>
> Types of provision: ....
>
> Based on your chosen types of provision, write notes in the table below before answering the question.
>
> | Similarities | Differences |
> |---|---|
> | | |
> | | |
> | | |

Photocopying prohibited   7

Now write your answer.

....
....
....
....
....
....
....
....
....
....

2 Nasreen is a teaching assistant who has worked in a secondary school for several years. Nasreen is eager to progress in her career and has been considering her options for professional growth.

Discuss **two** potential options she could explore to further her career in a secondary school setting.

Your response should demonstrate:

▷ the advantages and disadvantages of each option

▷ recommendations based on her goals and the broader educational context.

(12 marks, plus 3 marks for QWC)

Plan your own answer

Complete the table below to plan your answer before writing – then use each box in the table to support you to write a paragraph for each option.

Career option	Advantages	Disadvantages

Now write your answer.

....
....
....
....
....
....
....
....
....
....

3 A nursery school has decided to employ a Physical Activity and Nutrition Coordinator (PANCo) to add extra support to the early years department in the school.

Discuss this specialist role and its responsibilities.

Your response should demonstrate understanding of:

▷ the expected impact of the role in supporting children's health and wellbeing.

(12 marks, plus 3 marks for QWC)

....
....
....
....
....
....
....
....
....
....
....
....
....
....

Education and Early Years T Level Exam Practice Workbook

Chapter 2 Supporting Education

Recall activities

1 Complete the following sentences on the Early Years Foundation Stage (EYFS).

   a The EYFS framework sets the standards for learning, development and care for children from .... to .... years.

   b There are .... areas of learning and development within the EYFS.

   c These are split into two sections: p............................ areas and s............................ areas.

   d There are .... p............................ areas and .... s............................ areas.

   e Each area has a range of .... Goals that children are expected to achieve at the end of the reception year.

2 Name the **three** characteristics of effective teaching within the EYFS.

   1) Playing and ....

   2) .... learning

   3) .... and ....

3 Complete the following table on the four Key Stages of the National Curriculum.

Key stage	Year group	Age
	Nursery Reception class	0–5 years
Key Stage 1	Years 1 and 2	
Key Stage 2		
Key Stage 3		
Key Stage 4		

10   **Photocopying prohibited**

4 a Complete the mind map on the professional behaviours teachers and practitioners must demonstrate that are essential for supporting children's education.

> **Tip**
> One professional behaviour has been completed for you. Can you think of at least five other behaviours?

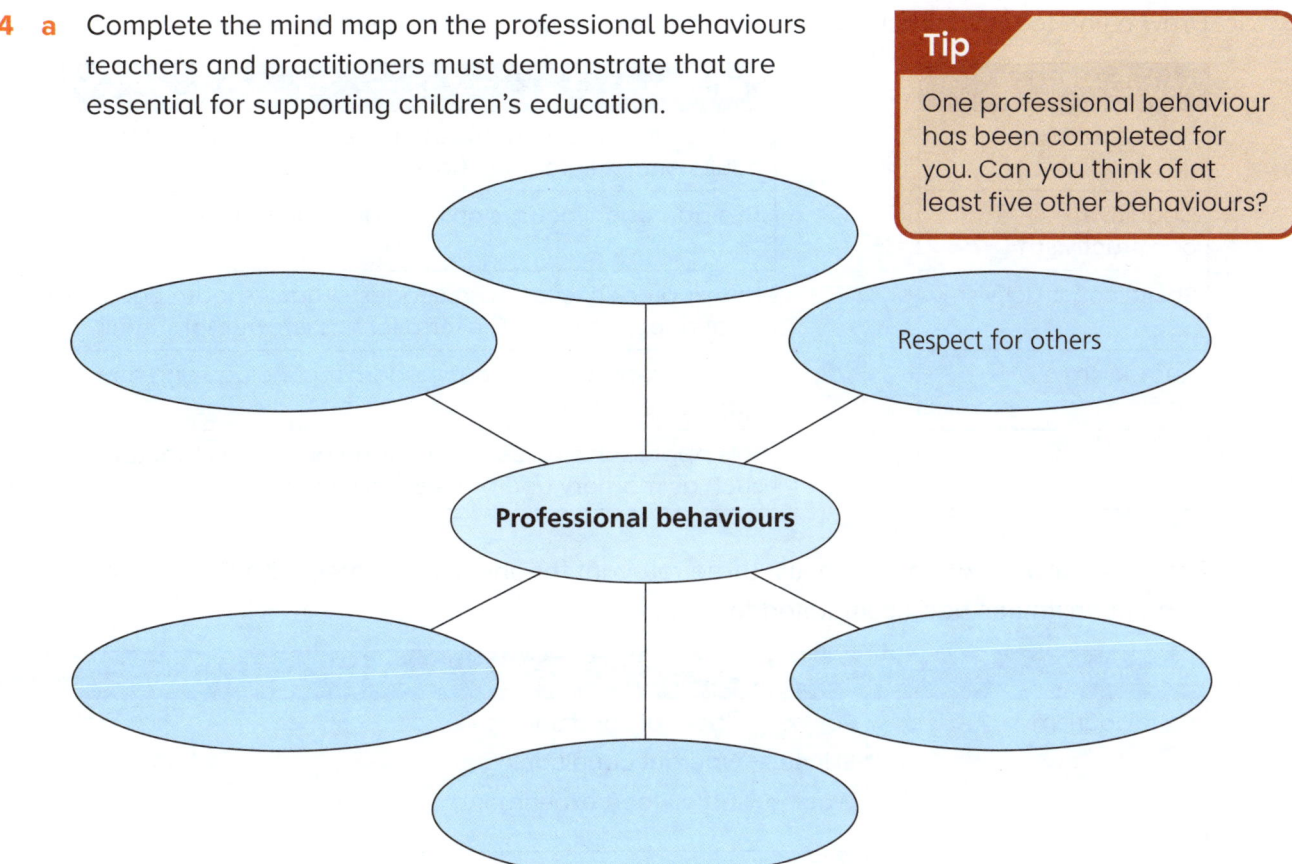

b List why the five behaviours from your mind map in Part **a** are important when supporting children and young people in their education. An example has been completed for you.

Behaviour	Importance in supporting children and young people
Respect for others	Helps to build positive relationships with children which can help with motivation and behaviour – children will also be able to model this behaviour

5 a Draw a line to match each theoretical educational approach to its definition.

Approach	Definition
Behaviourism	This approach concentrates on the interactions between adults and children and how they support learning.
Cognitive constructivism	This approach focuses on feelings and attitudes.
Social constructivism	This approach to learning suggests that we learn because of what happens to us. The term for this is 'external stimuli'.
Humanism	This approach is all about modern technology and how it can support learning.
Connectivism	This approach stresses the thinking processes that take place, such as memory and processing information.

b For each theoretical approach, list three relevant theorists associated with that approach. Behaviourism has been completed for you.

Approach	Theorist
Behaviourism	Pavlov – Classical conditioning Skinner – Operant conditioning Watson – Little Albert experiment
Cognitive constructivism	
Social constructivism	
Humanism	
Connectivism	

Chapter 2 Supporting Education

Short-answer exam-style practice questions

1. Which of the following is a prime area of the EYFS? (1 mark)

   A Mathematics ☐

   B Literacy ☐

   C Understanding of the world ☐

   D Communication and language ☐

2. Which assessment is completed on each child at the beginning of a reception class? (1 mark)

   A Two-year check ☐

   B Assessment for learning (AfL) ☐

   C Early Years Foundation Stage Profile (EYFSP) ☐

   D Reception Baseline Assessment (RBA) ☐

3. Which theorist studied children's copying behaviour and named his theory 'social cognitive theory'? (1 mark)

   A Piaget ☐

   B Bandura ☐

   C Watson ☐

   D Skinner ☐

4. State what is referred to as the 'microsystem' according to Bronfenbrenners' bioecological system. (2 marks)

   ....

   ....

5. Describe the model of 'operant conditioning' and how it relates to how children learn behaviour in schools. (4 marks)

   ....

   ....

   ....

   ....

   ....

6 According to Piaget, children at a certain age assume their thoughts and feelings are the same as everyone else's and do not understand any other perspective apart from their own.

Identify what he called this action **and** at what age and stage of his stages of development does this occur? (2 marks)

....

....

7 a Identify **one** advocate of the humanist approach. (1 mark)

b Outline **two** key features of the example that you have given in Part **a**. (2 marks)

> **Sample answer**
> a Maslows' hierarchy of needs
> b Maslow stressed the importance of fulfilling children's basic needs so they can reach their full potential. Maslow also said they can then focus on self-actualisation.
>
> **Analysis**
> The first part of the student's response gives a good example of a humanist approach. The second part clearly states the key principles of the approach. This answer is likely to be awarded the full 3 marks.

Can you think of another advocate of the humanist approach that you could use to answer this question?

a ....

b ....

....

8 Describe **two** personal factors that could affect a child's engagement in literacy. (4 marks)

> **Hint**
> Which particular individual need or ability could affect children in either a positive or negative way? Also consider their motivation and previous experience in relation to developing those skills.

Chapter 2 Supporting Education

Long-answer exam-style practice questions

1. Luca is seven years old and attends the local primary school. Luca can often loose motivation and finds learning literacy difficult.

   a Describe **two** different factors that could be affecting Luca's engagement in learning. (4 marks)

   > **Hint**
   >
   > Consider the personal, environmental and educational factors that could be affecting Luca's engagement.

   ....

   ....

   ....

   ....

   ....

   ....

   b Identify **one** strategy Luca's teacher could implement to support his learning. (2 marks)

   ....

   ....

2. Nursery staff want to enhance their skills in creating a language-rich environment to support the development of their learners. The nursery has a diverse group of children, each with unique language backgrounds and abilities.

   Nursery manager Collete is committed to providing opportunities for professional growth and development. She has organised a staff development day dedicated to enhancing language-rich environments in the nursery classroom.

   Discuss how the staff can work together to set up a language-rich environment for the new class **and** the importance of involving all staff members in the planning and implementation process.

   Include evidence of demonstrating reasoned justifications of the following:

   ▷ understanding of activities and resources that can be used to support language development in a nursery classroom

   ▷ strategies for how the nursery staff can facilitate language development through interactions, play and structured activities

   ▷ knowledge of a theory that identifies the importance of the adult in the environment supporting learning.

   (12 marks, plus 3 marks for QWC)

Photocopying prohibited   15

Education and Early Years T Level Exam Practice Workbook

> **Plan your own answer**
>
> Use this table to help plan your ideas before writing your answer. It is set up to support you to structure your answer. Each section could be used as a starting point to write a paragraph to cover the points that need answering.
>
> Remember, 3 marks will be given to the quality of your writing so remember to check through what you have written for this longer question.

How practitioners can work together	
Activities and resources	
Adult role in the environment	
Relevant theory	

Now have a go at the answer.

....
....
....
....
....
....
....
....
....
....
....
....
....

Chapter 2 Supporting Education

3 Henry is a Level 3 practitioner at a nursery school and has enrolled on an online foundation degree course in Early Childhood Studies. He has chosen an online course as it fits in better with his work and home life commitments. He is hoping the course will lead to further career opportunities.

Analyse this type of pedagogical approach to learning and how it will support Henry.

Your response should demonstrate understanding of:

▷ a specific connectivism theory that relates to the example above

▷ analysis of the strengths and weakness to learning in this particular way.

(12 marks, plus 3 marks for QWC)

....
....
....
....
....
....
....
....
....
....
....
....
....
....
....
....
....
....
....
....
....
....
....
....

4 Rosa is a five-year-old child who sometimes struggles to complete puzzles and tasks. She often becomes frustrated with herself in these situations.

Explain how metacognition strategies support children and young people like Rosa to manage their learning.

Your response should include understanding of the following:

▷ a clear definition of metacognition

▷ how metacognition helps support self-regulation and learning.

(12 marks, plus 3 marks for QWC)

Chapter 3 Safeguarding, Health and Safety and Wellbeing

Recall activities

1. Write a definition for the term 'safeguarding'.

   ....

2. It is important that anyone working with children understands statutory guidance in relation to safeguarding, health and safety and wellbeing.

   Complete the mind map below with names of relevant guidance. An example has been given to start you off.

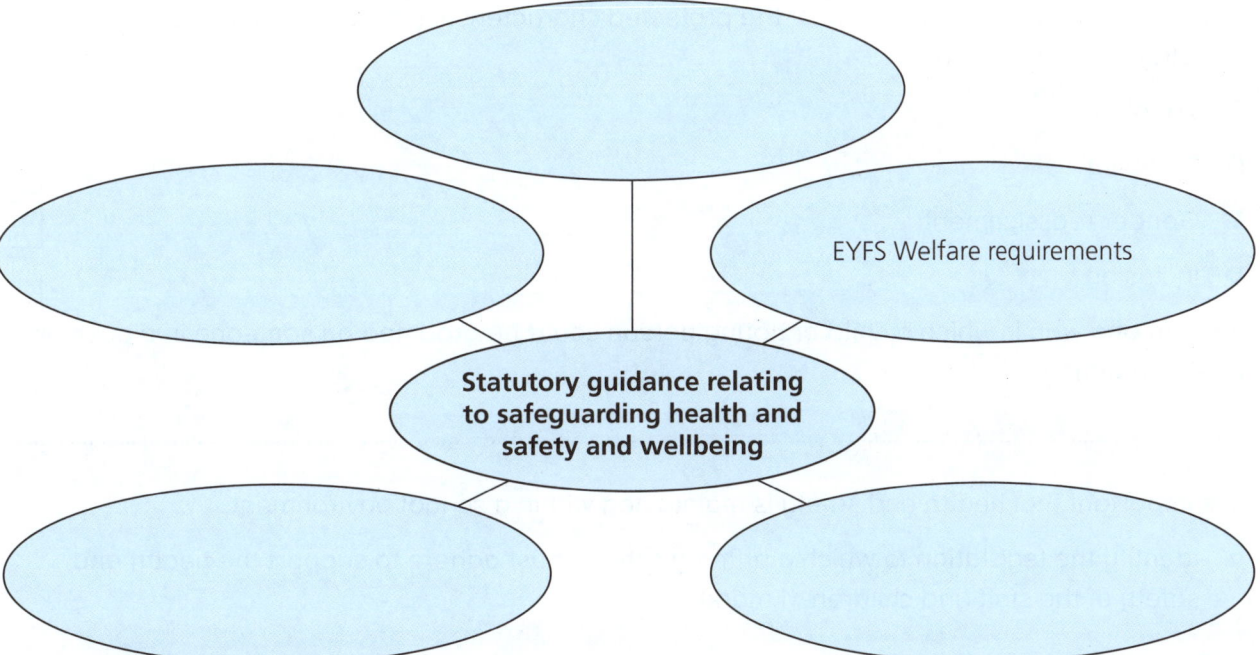

3. Draw a line to match each breach of a position of trust by an adult to its example.

How adults may use power and influence to abuse children	Example
Using a position of trust to bully, humiliate or undermine.	A member of school staff exploits a child for their own benefit.
Threatening punishment for non-compliance with unreasonable demands.	A teaching assistant accesses personal information on a child so that they can contact them outside of school.
Take advantage of an individual.	A teacher consistently bullies a child in front of other pupils in the class.
Gain unauthorised access to private information for their own advantage.	A child's teacher threatens to hurt a child if they do not agree to specific demands.

4   Write out the full title for the following acronyms that relate to safeguarding children.

GDPR	
LAC	
FGM	
DSL	
CSE	

Short-answer exam-style practice questions

1   Which one of the following is one of the protected characteristics as identified in the Equality Act 2010? (1 mark)

   A   Equality ☐

   B   Diversity ☐

   C   Gender reassignment ☐

   D   Inclusion ☐

2   Identify **one** way in which a child or young person could be groomed by someone in a position of trust. (1 mark)

   ....

3   It is important that health and safety is maintained within a school environment.

   a   Identify the legislation to which a primary school must adhere to support the health and safety of the staff and children. (1 mark)

   ....

   b   Describe **two** procedures that the school would need to put in place to meet this legislation. (2 marks)

   > **Hint**
   >
   > Think about the procedures that were in place at your placement – which ones are there to protect the health and safety of everyone (staff and children)?

   ....

   ....

   ....

   ....

Chapter 3 Safeguarding, Health and Safety and Wellbeing

4 Identify **three** reasons why secondary school teachers must maintain compliance with General Data Protection Regulations (GDPR) as set out in the Data Protection Act 2018. (3 marks)

....

....

....

....

....

....

5 Outline **three** factors that could indicate that a child is vulnerable or at risk of abuse. (3 marks)

....

....

....

....

....

....

6 Describe the difference between a child or young person who is 'in need' and a child or young person who is 'at risk'. (4 marks)

....

....

....

....

....

....

....

....

7 Describe **two** procedures that a primary school should have in place to support the settings' safeguarding policy. (4 marks)

> **Sample answer**
> All staff would need to have a DBS to work with children. All staff should follow the safeguarding policy.
>
> **Analysis**
> Although this answer is correct it would require more detail to gain full marks, including:
> ▶ who else, as well as the staff, would need a DBS (Disclosure and Barring Service) check and what type of DBS it should be
> ▶ identify and describe a second procedure that would be in the safeguarding policy.

Have a go at writing a stronger answer with these points in mind.

....
....
....
....
....
....
....
....

8 a Define the term 'position of trust'. (1 mark)

....
....

b A nursery teacher ensures the safety and emotional well-being of the children by constantly providing a nurturing environment and listening to their concerns. Describe what else the nursery teacher might do to keep the 'position of trust'. (2 marks)

....
....
....

Chapter 3 Safeguarding, Health and Safety and Wellbeing

Long-answer exam-style practice questions

1 Nicola is a nursery practitioner. She notices some concerning behaviour in a four-year-old child who has been attending the nursery for over a year.

Lately, the child has become withdrawn and is often seen playing alone during group activities. She seems unusually quiet and avoids eye contact with both peers and nursery staff. She has been drawing pictures at the art table that depict violence and explosions. This is a significant change from her previous behaviour, where she was sociable and had a positive attitude.

Discuss what Nicola should do about her concerns.

Your answer should demonstrate understanding of:

▷ how Nicola should approach the situation regarding the child's change in behaviour

▷ what initial steps Nicola would take to assess and address the child's wellbeing.

(12 marks, plus 3 marks for QWC)

> **Hint**
>
> Review the concerns that Nicola has identified – How does she need to act? What policy and procedures should she immediately follow?

2 In a local secondary school, staff are concerned as they have dealt with two serious bullying incidents in the past two weeks. The second case is related to cyberbullying through social media.

Discuss how this situation could be addressed.

Your answer should demonstrate understanding of:

▷ the short-term and long-term effects of bullying on a child or young person, considering both academic and emotional effects

▷ possible strategies that the school could implement to aim to prevent bullying, particularly cyberbullying, in the school environment.

(12 marks, plus 3 marks for QWC)

> **Plan your own answer**
> There are two points to consider for this question:
>
> **Effects of bullying:** Write some ideas in the table.
>
> | Short-term effects of the bullying | Long-term effects of the bullying |
> |---|---|
> | | |
>
> **Strategies to prevent bullying:** Write some ideas in the table.
>
> | Short-term solutions | Long-term solutions |
> |---|---|
> | | |

Using your notes from the table write your answer to the question.

3 Sasha is a 15-year-old secondary school student. Her form teacher, Mr Thacker, a 30-year-old male, has been identified as engaging in an inappropriate relationship with Sasha. He and Sasha have been seen spending an unusual amount of time together inside and outside of school and there have been reports of private texting and social media interactions. Two staff members have raised concerns about inappropriate communication and possible grooming behaviours.

Discuss how this should be dealt with.

Your answer should demonstrate understanding of:

▷ the potential indicators of an inappropriate relationship between a school staff member and a child

▷ why it is essential for childcare professionals to be vigilant in identifying signs of inappropriate relationships

▷ the steps that should be taken to ensure the child's safety and the legal obligations of the school.

(12 marks, plus 3 marks for QWC)

Chapter 4 Behaviour

Recall activities

1 Fill in the chart to identify how stages of social, emotional and physical development may impact behaviour. One example has been added to get you started.

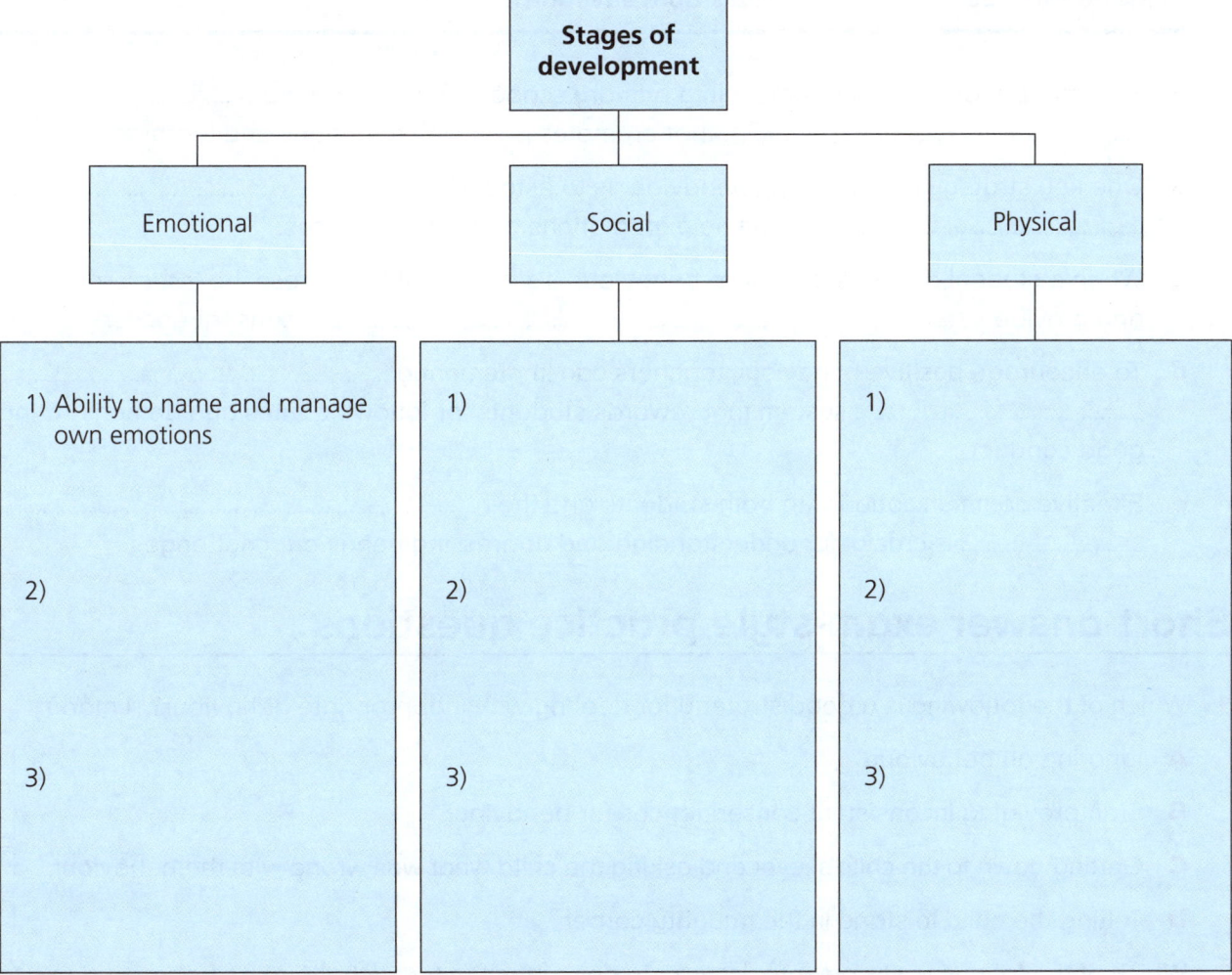

Stages of development

Emotional
1) Ability to name and manage own emotions
2)
3)

Social
1)
2)
3)

Physical
1)
2)
3)

2 Fill in the table below to complete the definitions for the three elements that inform children's/young people's self-concept. Part of the table has been completed already.

Element	Definition
1) Self-image	
2) Self-esteem	
3)	How you would like to be

3 List **one** positive and **one** negative impact of behaviour on a young person's self-concept.

Positive: ....

Negative: ....

4 Fill in the blanks to complete each sentence on behaviour management.

Use this list of words:

> reinforcement   parents and carers   consistent
> classroom rules   classroom environment

- **a** Effective behaviour management in a primary school involves creating a .... that promotes positive interactions and learning.

- **b** One key strategy for managing behaviour is to establish clear .... that outline expectations and consequences.

- **c** When a student displays disruptive behaviour, it's important to address the issue promptly and provide .... consequences.

- **d** To encourage positive behaviour, teachers can implement a .... system that rewards students for following rules and demonstrating good conduct.

- **e** Effective communication with both students and their .... is crucial for understanding and addressing behaviour challenges.

Short-answer exam-style practice questions

1 Which of the following is a good strategy for dealing with inappropriate behaviour? (1 mark)

- **A** Ignoring all behaviour.
- **B** Staff providing inconsistent consequences for behaviour.
- **C** Getting down to the child's level and asking the child what was wrong with the behaviour.
- **D** Telling the child to stand in the naughty corner.

2 Which of the following statements accurately describes the term 'challenging behaviour' in a childcare setting? (1 mark)

- **A** Challenging behaviour refers exclusively to physical aggression and violence displayed by children.
- **B** Challenging behaviour encompasses a wide range of actions that may disrupt learning or social interactions.
- **C** Challenging behaviour is limited to behaviours exhibited by children only; adults cannot display challenging behaviours.
- **D** Challenging behaviour is a rare occurrence and usually indicates a serious developmental disorder.

Chapter 4 Behaviour

3 A range of factors can affect children and young people's behaviour in different ways.

  a Outline **two** individual factors that could positively affect behaviour. (4 marks)

  ....
  ....
  ....
  ....
  ....
  ....
  ....

  b Outline **one** educational factor that could negatively affect behaviour. (2 mark)

  ....

  ....

  ....

  ....

  ....

> **Tip**
> Consider how peer relationships could have an influence on a child in a learning environment.

4 Explain **two** strategies that would support children and young people to develop self-regulation and resilience. (4 marks)

> **Tip**
> The question is asking for two strategies – make sure that you write two and explain them in detail for the full marks.

  ....

  ....

  ....

  ....
  ....
  ....
  ....
  ....
  ....

5 Describe **two** key reasons why a school should have a detailed behaviour policy. (4 marks)

....

....

....

....

....

....

6 Describe **two** ways adults can use non-verbal communication to maintain positive behaviour in children and young people. (4 marks)

> **Sample answer**
>
> Non-verbal communication could be body language and facial expressions.
>
> **Comments**
>
> Do you think this answer gives clear examples of non-verbal communication? Is it written in enough detail to gain 2 full marks for each point? Can you think of any other ways of using verbal or non-verbal communication? How could you write the responses more clearly – write some notes here before attempting your own answer.
>
> ....
>
> ....
>
> ....
>
> ....

Now write your own answer.

....

....

....

....

....

....

....

Long-answer exam-style practice questions

1 A primary school headteacher has called a staff meeting to address the issue of challenging behaviour that has started to surface within Year 5 and 6 children at lunch and break times.

   Explain why it is important that this challenging behaviour is addressed **and** what the staff will need to do to assess the risks to themselves and others when dealing with this challenging behaviour. (6 marks)

   > **Hint**
   >
   > It is important to mention the setting's policies and procedures within your answer.

   ....
   ....
   ....
   ....
   ....
   ....
   ....
   ....
   ....
   ....
   ....
   ....
   ....
   ....

2 Joelle is a 15-year-old who has been struggling with her self-image lately. She often expresses dissatisfaction with her appearance and compares herself negatively to her peers on social media. This has led to a decline in her self-esteem and overall confidence. She has started avoiding social gatherings and extracurricular activities she used to enjoy. Joelle's parents are concerned about her wellbeing and have approached the class teacher for guidance on how to support her in improving her self-image and self-esteem.

   Discuss how the school can directly assist Joelle in building a healthier self-image.

   Your response should consider:

   ▷ the potential factors that might contribute to Joelle's negative self-image

   ▷ the importance of working in partnership with parents

   ▷ strategies to support Joelle's parents to help improve her self-image and self-esteem.

   (12 marks Plus 3 marks for QWC)

> **Sample answer**
>
> Joelle's negative self-image could be influenced by various factors. Firstly, the influence of social media can lead her to developing unrealistic ideals of beauty. Secondly, peer pressure, especially on social media, can create feelings of inadequacy as she constantly compares herself to others.
>
> **Comments**
>
> This is a student's first paragraph and only covers the first discussion point. The student has identified social media as a significant factor in many teenagers' lives and the explanation provides a clear understanding of how this factor affects Joelle.
>
> It mentions that Joelle might internalise unrealistic beauty ideals, which is a common consequence of exposure to media portrayals of beauty. This is an accurate and relevant point. The explanation expands on how peer comparison, especially on social media, can impact Joelle's self-esteem. This is a well-articulated explanation that demonstrates an understanding of the issue.

Plan your own answer

- To gain full marks, you will need to address all the bullet points in detail.
- Consider how for each bullet point you can demonstrate your wider understanding. Give specific examples for each element.

Now write your own answer.

3 Isha is two years old and attends a day-care centre. She has been at the centre for a few months now and is gradually adjusting to the new environment. However, staff have noticed some challenging behaviours related to self-regulation, especially during transitions and meals. She becomes upset when it is time to stop playing with her toys and move on to another activity, such as circle time or snack time. During meals, Isha has difficulty sitting still in her chair and tends to get frustrated when she has to wait for her food.

Discuss the approach that can be taken to address this situation.

Your answer should demonstrate understanding of:

▷ the reasons Isha may be having difficulty transitioning from one activity to another

▷ the strategies that practitioners at the day-care setting could use to support Isha during transitions

▷ the reason Isha may exhibit challenging behaviour during mealtimes and how it can be addressed.

(12 marks, plus 3 marks for QWC)

Chapter 5 Parents, Families and Carers

Recall activities

1 Draw a line between the type of family and the corresponding definition.

Term	Definition
Nuclear family	Where one parent, either a mother or a father, is responsible for raising the child or children on their own.
Extended family	Formed when two parents with children from previous relationships come together and create a new family unit.
Single-parent family	Consists of two parents (usually a mother and a father) and their biological or adopted children, living together in the same household.
Blended family	A temporary family arrangement where children who cannot live with their birth parents are placed under the care of foster parents or guardians.
Foster family	Includes not only parents and children but also grandparents, aunts, uncles and cousins, often living in the same household or in close proximity.

2 Fill in the blanks with the correct parenting style to complete the sentences. Choose the parenting styles from the options provided below.

> **Helicopter**　**Instinctive**　**Permissive**
> **Uninvolved**　**Authoritarian**　**Authoritative**

a ……………………………………………… parents set clear rules and expectations for their children while also being responsive and nurturing. They provide guidance and support, encouraging independence and self-discipline.

b ……………………………………………… parents are very lenient and have few demands or restrictions on their children. They are often indulgent and avoid using discipline.

c ……………………………………………… parents are overly involved and overly protective. They like to 'hover' over their children.

d ……………………………………………… parents are strict and controlling, with high demands and little responsiveness to their children's needs. They expect obedience without question.

e ……………………………………………… parents are emotionally distant in their children's lives. They provide minimal guidance, attention and support.

f ……………………………………………… parents are hard-wired to be able to be parents and to understand how to be parents. They rely on instinct and intuition.

Education and Early Years T Level Exam Practice Workbook

Short-answer exam-style practice questions

1. Which **one** of the following professionals mainly works with parents/carers with children 0–5 years? (1 mark)

   A Area SENDCO ☐

   B Social worker ☐

   C Health visitor ☐

   D Speech and language therapist ☐

2. List **two** ways settings can communicate and share information with parents, carers and families. (2 marks)

   > **Sample answer**
   >
   > A setting could talk to the parents when they pick the child up or drop them off at the setting. In my placement they also send out a weekly letter.
   >
   > **Comments**
   >
   > Do you think these are good examples? What ways have you seen parents included in the school environment in your placement or when you were at school?
   >
   > ....
   >
   > ....

   Now write your own answer.

   ....

   ....

   ....

   ....

3. Describe **two** ways that a primary school can invite parents, carers and families to get involved within the school environment. (2 marks)

   > **Tip**
   >
   > Highlight the key points in the question before answering. Question 3 needs **two** points for full marks and the answer must focus on a **primary school** environment.

   ....

   ....

   ....

   ....

Long-answer exam-style practice questions

1 Sofia is a single mother of a four-year-old boy, Jacob, who attends preschool. Jacob is a creative and energetic child who loves exploring new activities. Since the beginning of the school year, Sofia has been somewhat distant and less involved in the school community compared to other parents. She rarely attends parent–teacher meetings or school events. She seems preoccupied and reluctant to engage in conversations about Jacob's progress and wellbeing.

   a State why it is important that educators are sensitive and mindful of different family contexts and backgrounds. (2 marks)

   > **Hint**
   > Focus your response on the age of the child and the type of setting.

   ....

   ....

   ....

   ....

   b Explain **two** potential barriers that might be preventing Sofia from participating in partnership activities with the preschool. (4 marks)

   ....

   ....

   ....

   ....

   ....

   ....

   ....

   c Discuss **three** strategies to foster a positive and effective partnership with Sofia to encourage her to become more engaged within the preschool. (6 marks)

   > **Plan your answer to Part c**
   > Fill in the table to plan the three strategies to encourage Sofia to become more engaged within the preschool. Think about relevant theories and practical examples you could mention. Reflect on strategies you may have seen used in your placement.

Strategy	How it will support effective partnership
1) Open door policy	Invite Sofia and other parents to attend an open morning in the preschool with a range of activities. Encourages time to talk/build relationship
2)	
3)	

Use the information from the table to structure your answer.

....

....

....

....

....

....

....

....

....

2 Jonathon is a dedicated early years practitioner working at a local childcare setting that provides care and education for children aged from two to five years. Jonathon understands the importance of collaboration between early years practitioners, parents, carers and families to support the holistic development of the children in his care.

Assess the impact of developing positive relationships with parents, carers and families.

Your response should demonstrate:

▷ why collaboration between early years practitioners and parents/carers is essential for supporting children's development

▷ the advantages of involving families in the learning process and activities at a childcare setting

▷ how early years practitioners can work with families to promote parental engagement/involvement.

(12 marks, plus 3 marks for QWC)

> **Tip**
>
> Underline the key points in the scenario and question before starting your answer – this will help keep your response focused.

Chapter 6 Working with Others

Recall activities

1. Complete the following table by identifying five types of professionals who may support children, parents, carers and families and stating what their role is.

   One example has been added to get you started.

Specialist support professional	Role in supporting children, carers and families
Educational psychologist	Work in the community and the educational system

2. Complete the mind map of what to consider when collaboratively working with other agencies and professionals. One is filled in for you.

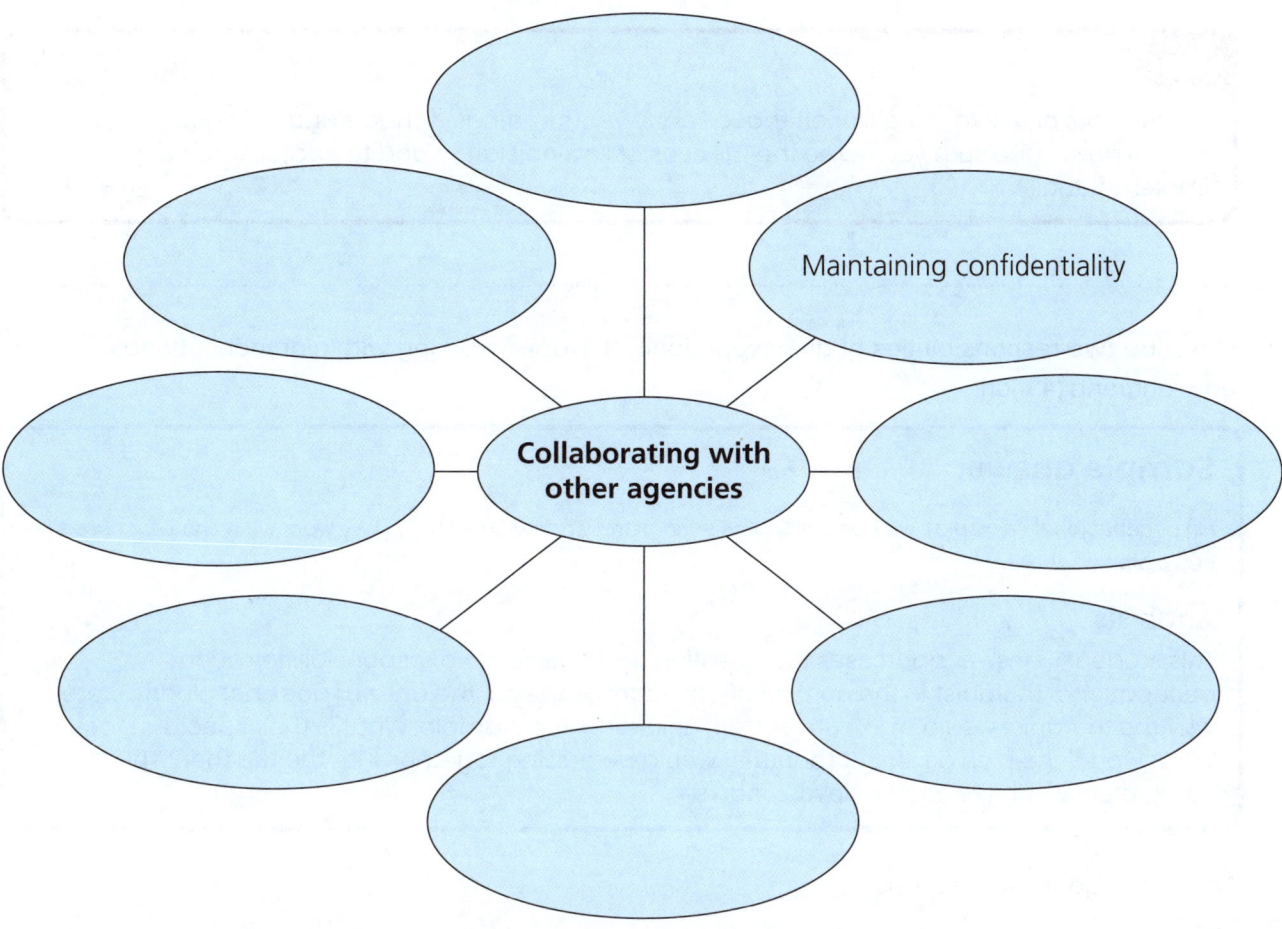

Short-answer exam-style practice questions

1. Which **one** of the following communication strategies is crucial for effective teamwork? (1 mark)
   - A Competing for ideas and solutions
   - B Avoiding sharing information with others
   - C Listening actively to understand perspectives
   - D Restricting communication to email only

2. Why is continuous professional development (CPD) important for effective collaborative work with other professionals in childcare settings? (1 mark)
   - A It is mandatory to meet regulatory requirements.
   - B It helps maintain a competitive edge over other professionals.
   - C It allows practitioners to keep updated with best practices and knowledge sharing.
   - D It ensures a hierarchy within the team based on the level of training attained.

3 State the name of the legislation in place to protect personal information and data and privacy? (1 mark)

> **Tip**
>
> There is lots of relevant legislation that all early years settings, schools and colleges must follow. Make sure you revise the full titles of key legislation and the dates they were implemented.

....

4 Describe **two** responsibilities of an occupational therapist working within an educational environment. (4 marks)

> **Sample answer**
>
> *An occupational therapist will come into the school and work with a child. They work with the teachers to put a plan together.*
>
> **Analysis**
>
> This student's answer addresses the question and outlines two responsibilities of an occupational therapist in the context of childcare. However, the answer does not clearly state why the therapist would work with certain children – for example: What is their specialist focus? What would the plan be about that they would be putting together with the teacher? This sample answer is likely to achieve 2 marks.

Now write your own answer.

....
....
....
....
....
....

5 Primary school teachers work collaboratively with other agencies and professionals to achieve better outcomes for children.

Explain how collaborative working achieves better outcomes for children. (4 marks)

> **Hint**
>
> Focus on agencies and professionals who would work collaboratively with teachers within a **primary** school, for example, school nurse or speech and language therapist.

Long-answer exam-style practice questions

1 Alma is a Level 3 childcare learner who works at a local day-care centre. A child at the day-care called Liam struggles with sensory processing difficulties; he becomes overwhelmed during group activities and has difficulty regulating his emotions. Alma recognises the importance of collaborating with other professionals to provide the best support for Liam's development and wellbeing.

   a Identify **two** professionals that Alma could work with to best support Liam's development and wellbeing. (2 marks)

   b Describe **two** ways maintaining professional boundaries with these professionals working with Liam will impact Alma's learning and practice. (4 marks)

   > **Hint**
   >
   > Alma is a Level 3 learner: consider the long-term impact on her learning and practice. Give specific examples of the impact on her future practice. You may be able to link this to your own development in placement when working with other internal and external professionals.

c   Explain why it is important for practitioners like Alma to establish professional relationships with internal and external professionals when supporting children with particular needs such as Liam. (6 marks)

> **Sample answer**
>
> c   If the staff like Alma are working with other professionals, they will then be able to support all the needs of Liam and help his holistic development and sensory needs. The staff will be able to learn from the other professionals and it will help their training and development. They can add it to their CPD log. They will be able share this with the other practitioners.
>
> **Comments**
>
> This student's answer provides an overview of the importance of professional relationships when working with children like Liam. However, a stronger answer would elaborate more, use examples and have a balanced view by addressing potential long-term benefits as well. This would demonstrate a deeper understanding of the subject and contribute to a more comprehensive response. This response is likely to gain 2 out of 6 marks.

Now write your own answer.

2. During playtime at a day nursery, Sonali notices that a child, Adeeva, who is usually active and sociable, seems withdrawn and disinterested. She does not want to participate in the activities and often sits alone, appearing sad.

Sonali thinks there may be underlying issues affecting Adeeva's emotional wellbeing. Sonali feels that Adeeva might benefit from professional support outside the childcare setting.

Discuss what Sonali should do to support the situation.

Your response should demonstrate:

- understanding of the steps Sonali should take to address Adeeva's situation while maintaining confidentiality
- understanding of the process of making a referral for Adeeva and the importance of obtaining parental consent in such situations
- reasoned judgements on why it is essential for childcare practitioners to work with other professionals when dealing with concerns about a child's emotional wellbeing.

(12 marks, plus 3 marks for QWC)

Chapter 7 Child Development

Recall activities

1 Physical development skills can be broken down into two types:

   a .... motor skills

   b .... motor skills

2 List the **three** concepts of John Bowlby's attachment theory. Give an example for each concept.

	Key concept	Example of concept
1	Innate attachment to one figure	
2		
3		

3 Identify **three** bodily changes that happen to males and females during puberty.

Males	Females

4 List **four** gross motor skill milestones for a child aged between six weeks to two years. Include approximate ages for the milestones.

Milestone	Age

5 a Complete the sentence:

A transition in a child's or young person's life is ....

....

....

....

b Complete the mind map to identify a range of unexpected transitions. One has been done for you.

> **Tip**
> Try to think of five other unexpected transitions.

- Unexpected transitions
  - Bereavement

Short-answer exam-style practice questions

1 At what age might a child be able to sit up alone? (1 mark)

   A 3 months

   B 6 months

   C 9 months

   D 12 months

2 Which **one** of the following is a fine motor skill? (1 mark)

   A Jumping off a step with feet together

   B Riding a tricycle and steering

   C Putting on and fastening clothes

   D Kicking a ball gently

3   Which **one** of the following theorists' studies led to the creation of the Strange Situation experiment? (1 mark)

    A Rutter ☐

    B Bowlby ☐

    C Ainsworth ☐

    D Schaffer ☐

4   Which **one** of the following is a feature of Piaget's formal operational stage of development? (1 mark)

    A Use of complex thinking ☐

    B Use of symbolic thinking ☐

    C Use of adoptive thinking ☐

    D Use of abstract thinking ☐

5   Define the term 'expressive language' in terms of language acquisition. (1 mark)

....

....

6   Describe **two** ways that 'circle time' supports language development. (4 marks)

> **Sample answer**
>
> Circle time is good for children to talk about what they have been doing at the weekend and quiet children to be more confidence.
>
> **Analysis**
>
> Two good examples given in this response. However, the answer would benefit from more detail as this is a 'describe' question. Remember to check your work – the last sentence should read 'to be more confident'.

Now write your own answer

....

....

....

....

....

....

....

7 Describe the difference between expected and unexpected transitions. (4 marks)

....

....

....

....

....

8 Daniel is four years old and attends a nursery school. His mother has told the nursery that Daniel has a short stay in hospital coming up for a small operation.

  a Give **two** reasons why it is important that the practitioners work together with Daniels' mother to support this transition. (2 marks)

....

....

....

....

  b Discuss **two** ways that the practitioners can support Daniel to prepare for his hospital stay. (4 marks)

> **Hint**
>
> Daniel's mother may be anxious about this forthcoming event as well and Daniel may notice her anxiety.

....

....

....

....

....

....

9 Identify **two** biological factors and **two** environmental factors that can affect the speed of language acquisition. (4 marks)

> **Tip**
>
> For Question 9, remember to include two **different** factors for **each** component.

....

....

....

....

....

....

Chapter 7 Child Development

Long-answer exam-style practice questions

1 Layla is an early years practitioner in the baby room at a local day nursery where ages range from six weeks to 12 months. Layla needs to put together a plan of how she will support language development for the babies in her care.

Explain the importance of having a detailed understanding of language acquisition when working in early years settings.

Your response should demonstrate:

▷ understanding of language development from six weeks to 12 months and how babies acquire language

▷ knowledge of relevant strategies a practitioner can use to promote early language development

▷ understanding of a key theoretical perspective on the important role adults play in supporting babies and young children's language development.

(12 marks, plus 3 marks for QWC)

> **Plan your own answer**
>
> Look at the bullet points to know which key ideas you need to include in this answer. Then write a short plan for each bullet point.
>
> ▶ Understanding language development: it is important to give a range of development milestones and strategies within your response.
>
> ▶ Knowledge of relevant strategies: what the adult can do and when they can do it, and explain how it will support language. For example: *Practitioner can maintain eye contact/sing nursery rhymes while changing nappy/getting dressed – this will help them to stay focused and learn language.*
>
> Complete the table as a starting point.
>
> | Age | Language development milestones | Strategies |
> |---|---|---|
> | 6 weeks | Recognises parents voice and calms down | |
> | 3 months | | Maintain eye contact/facial expressions
Repetitive language |

Age	Language development milestones	Strategies
6 months	Blending vowels, babbling	
9 months		
12 months		Use of talk during routines

- ▶ Understanding the theoretical perspective: which theorist valued the role of the environment and the adults within it in supporting babies and young children acquiring language? Write some notes here.

....
....
....
....
....
....
....
....
....

Using your notes, now write your own answer.

2. Matthew is the deputy manager in a new baby unit and is developing training for his staff. He wants to focus a session on the work of Bowlby and attachment theory.

Assess Bowlby's studies on early attachments.

Your response should demonstrate:

▷ understanding of Bowlby's key concepts of attachment theory

▷ links between Bowlby's theory on maternal separation, three stages of separation anxiety and how to support the emotional wellbeing of babies

▷ reasoned judgements regarding the importance of his work in influencing practice in settings today.

(12 marks, plus 3 marks for QWC)

> **Tip**
>
> To gain the extra marks for quality of written communication (QWC), check that your answer:
> - is clearly expressed and well structured
> - has good grammar and spelling
> - uses a wide range of technical terms effectively.

Chapter 8 Observation and Assessment

Recall activities

1 Name the two types of assessment and give a definition for each:

   a F............................ assessments are ....

   ....

   b S............................ assessments are ....

   ....

2 Fill in the blanks in the flow diagram to complete the three stages of the planning cycle. Write the name of each stage and what a practitioner would do at each stage.

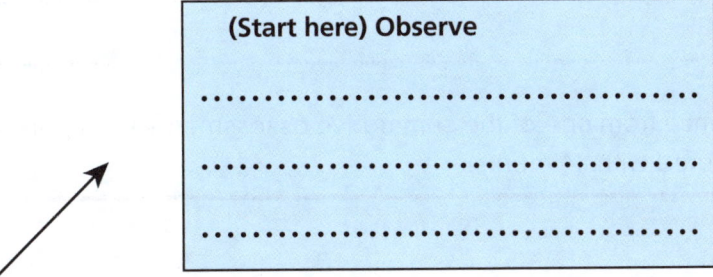

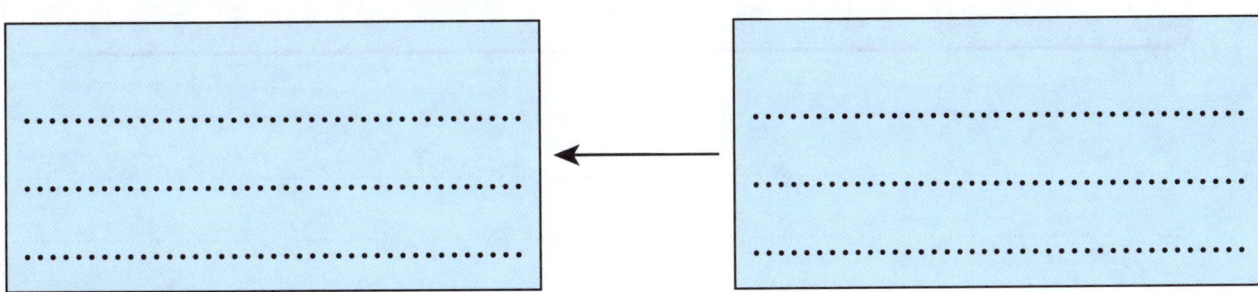

3 List **four** observation methods that can be used on children and **one** advantage of each method.

Method	Identify one advantage of method
1)	
2)	
3)	
4)	

Education and Early Years T Level Exam Practice Workbook

Short-answer exam-style practice questions

1 Which **one** of the following is responsible for conducting a Reception Baseline Assessment (RBA)? (1 mark)

   A Classroom assistant ☐
   B SENDCO ☐
   C Parent or carer ☐
   D Classroom teacher ☐

2 a Identify **two** summative assessments that need to be carried out as part of the Early Years Foundation Stage (EYFS). (2 marks)

   ....

   ....

   ....

   ....

   b Describe how the evidence from one of the summative assessments from part a) can be used and who it would be shared with. (4 marks)

   > **Hint**
   >
   > Consider what age the child would be when the summative assessment would be carried out and the benefit of it at this time.

   ....

   ....

   ....

   ....

   ....

   ....

3 Outline **two** differences between 'long/medium term' planning and 'in the moment' planning. (2 marks)

   ....

   ....

   ....

   ....

Photocopying prohibited

4 Identify **two** ways observations can be used to inform planning. (2 marks)

....

....

....

....

Long-answer exam-style practice questions

1 Rogan is an assessor who works with students in a further education (FE) college.

Evaluate the role of an assessor in assessing skills and progress and why it is important that the learners are observed in the workplace. (6 marks)

> **Hint**
>
> Evaluate what knowledge, skills and behaviours the assessor would be reviewing and why these observations would need to carried out on a regular basis.

....

....

....

....

....

....

....

....

....

....

....

....

....

....

....

....

....

2 Ruby is a new classroom assistant in a primary school setting. As part of her role, she needs to understand the different ongoing (formative) assessments that are carried out in the school. These assessments involve observing and documenting the progress of individual students.

Discuss the importance of conducting ongoing assessments on all children within this school.

In your response should also include:

▷ who these observations/assessments should be shared with, and why is it important to share this information with them

▷ where and how the assessments should be stored, and why this storage process is significant for the school and its students.

(12 marks, plus 3 marks for QWC)

> **Plan your own answer**
>
> Consider how these observations can be used:
> ▸ early intervention – identifying areas where students may struggle early on allows for timely intervention
> ▸ progress checking.
>
> Who can the assessments be passed onto:
> ▸ teachers – why?
> ▸ who else?
>
> Storage of assessments:
> ▸ what legislation and school policies/procedures does this link to?
>
> Write some notes here:

Using your plan, now write your answer.

3 Maria is a Level 3 childcare student working in a nursery setting that follows the EYFS framework. The nursery is currently exploring the theme of 'Animals and their Habitats'.

Discuss Maria's role in in the planning and assessment process to help the children achieve their learning objectives within this theme.

Your response should demonstrate:

▷ how the EYFS planning cycle can be applied to ensure that all children, regardless of their abilities and interests, make progress during the 'Animals and their Habitats' theme

▷ how the assessment information can be used to inform future planning and create a more individualised approach to meet the diverse needs of the children.

(12 marks, plus 3 marks for QWC)

Chapter 9 Reflective Practice

Recall activities

1 Complete the table with the missing stages of the Gibbs reflective cycle.

Stage	Name of stage	Describe the stage
1)	Description	What happened
2)		
3)	Evaluation	
4)		
5)	Conclusion	
6)		

2   Draw a line to connect the name of the stage in Kolb's experiential learning cycle and the corresponding definition.

Learning cycle stage
Concrete experience
Reflective observation of a new experience
Abstract conceptualisation
Active experimentation

Definition
When a practitioner has a new idea or has changed their thinking due to their experience.
When a practitioner encounters an activity or experience.
When a practitioner applies their new way of thinking for future experience.
Where a practitioner thinks back or reflects on their experience.

Short-answer exam-style practice questions

1   Which one of the following is the second stage of the Boud, Keogh and Walker model of reflection on practice? (1 mark)

   A   Evaluation

   B   Analysis

   C   Action plan

   D   Reflective process

2   Define the term 'Blended learning'. (1 mark)

   ....

3   Identify **two** advantages and **two** disadvantages of using technology in the classroom. (4 marks)

   > **Hint**
   > Consider all aspects of using technology and how it can support individuals learning and development, compared to limits on social interaction.

   Advantages: ....

   ....

   ....

   ....

   Disadvantages: ....

   ....

   ....

4 Describe what an appraisal is and why they are important. (3 marks)

> **Sample answer**
>
> An appraisal is an annual review that a practitioner would have with their line manager. At the meeting they would review what happened over the past year – for example, what went well and what could be improved on for the following year.
>
> **Analysis**
>
> This response clearly identifies what an appraisal is and what would be discussed in it. The answer would be stronger if it included information on how appraisals support the practitioner going forward. This would then answer the second part of the question (the importance of appraisals). The answer above is likely to gain 1 mark for answering the first part of the question.

Now write your own answer to the question.

....

....

....

....

....

....

Long-answer exam-style practice questions

1 Marco is an early years practitioner in a reception class. He is about to start working with a child, Alex, who has been diagnosed with autism spectrum condition (ASC) and experiences sensory sensitivities. He has previously had one-to-one support in the nursery attached to the school. Alex's parents have expressed their concerns about his challenges with communication and social interaction.

Describe why it is important that Marco uses reflective practice to develop his skills to support Alex and his family.

Your response should demonstrate:

▷ a discussion of the steps Marco could take to gather information about Alex's specific needs and preferences

▷ an understanding of what continuing professional development (CPD) Marco could take part in to improve his knowledge and developmental skills in order to support Alex.

(12 marks, plus 3 marks for QWC)

Plan your own answer

Use the tables to help you identify discussion points so that you cover both elements of the question.

Steps for gathering information on Alex's needs	How will it help?

CPD opportunities	How they will support Marco in his development
Shadowing another early years practitioner in the nursery	

Use your notes from the table to write your answer.

....
....
....
....
....
....
....
....
....
....

Chapter 9 Reflective Practice

2 Evaluate the pros and cons of using technology in the classroom to support learning. (12 marks, plus 3 marks for QWC)

> **Tip**
> 'Evaluating' means reviewing information and bringing it together to make a conclusion. Be sure to mention both the positives and negatives of using technology in the classroom to support learning. Make sure you show your understanding of what technology in the classroom is and use your experience from your placement when considering evidence for and against using technology to aid learning.

....
....
....
....
....
....
....
....
....
....
....
....
....
....
....
....
....
....
....
....
....
....

3 Ella is a practitioner in an early years childcare setting. She observes a group of children struggling with conflict resolution during playtime. As part of her role, Ella is responsible for guiding and supporting less experienced practitioners.

Discuss how Ella could provide guidance for these learners.

Your response should demonstrate:

▷ how Ella could apply reflective practice to analyse the situation involving the children's conflicts

▷ the value of CPD in the context of working in an early years setting

▷ the importance of collaboration with other practitioners within the early years childcare setting to support teamwork and personal development.

(12 marks, plus 3 marks for QWC)

> **Tip**
>
> Remember to plan your response – underline the key points in the scenario and the question before starting your answer.

Chapter 10 Equality and Diversity

Recall activities

1. Define the following terms.

Equality	
Diversity	
Inclusion	
Discrimination	

2. The United Nations Convention on the Rights of the Child (UNCRC) 1989 has four general principles. Complete the table on these articles.

Article number	Principle title	What it means
2		The UNCRC applies to every child without discrimination, whatever their ethnicity, sex, religion, language, abilities or any other status, whatever they think or say, whatever their family background.
	Best interest of the child	

Article number	Principle title	What it means
6		
	Right to be heard	Every child has the right to express their views, feelings and wishes in all matters affecting them, and to have their views considered and taken seriously.

3 Complete the mind map by naming a range of policies and procedures that a school would have relating to equality and diversity to comply with legal requirements. One has been done for you.

> **Tip**
>
> Can you think of at least five other policies? Think about what you may have learned or seen as part of your placement experience.

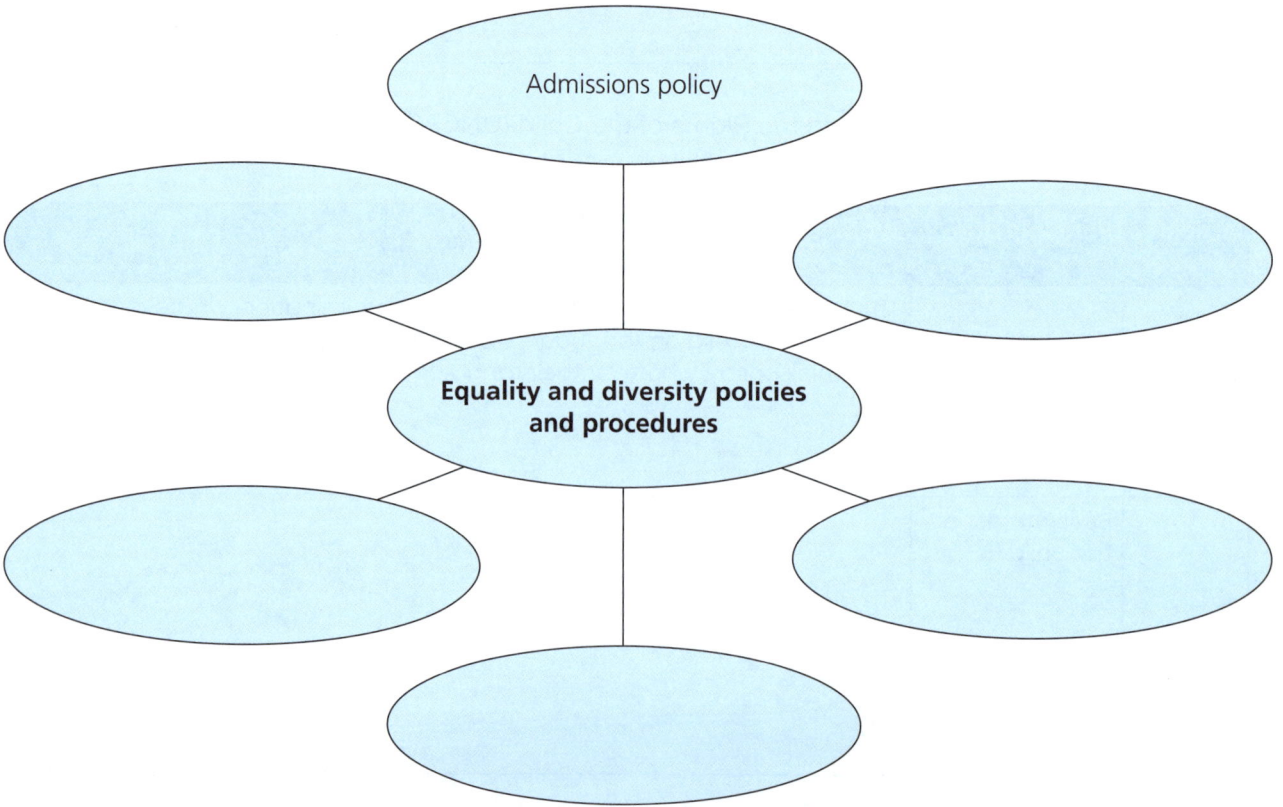

4 Complete the mind map to identify strategies that promote equality, diversity and inclusion in an educational environment. One has been done for you.

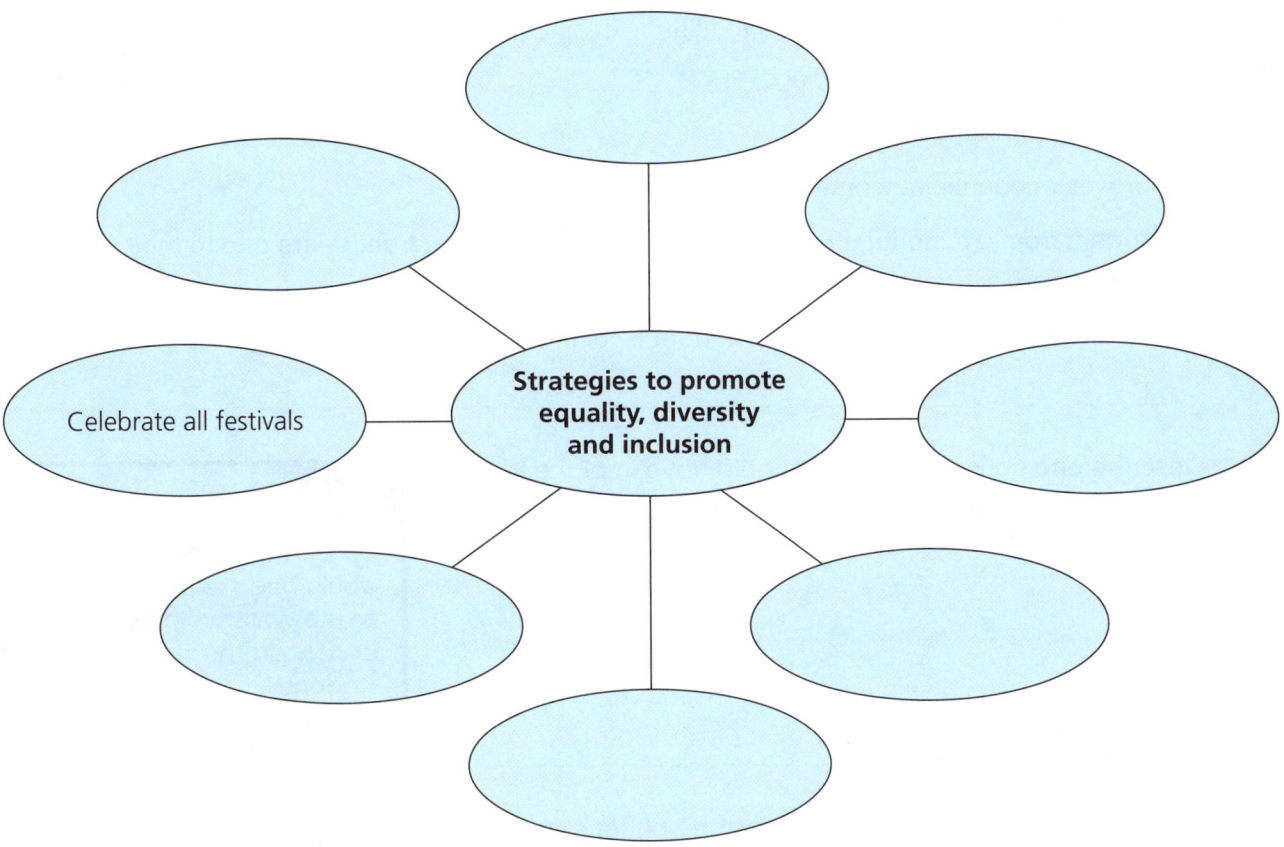

Short-answer exam-style practice questions

1 Which **one** of the following is a reason why is it important for Level 3 Childcare students to promote equality and diversity in their practice? (1 mark)

   A   It helps them secure better job opportunities.

   B   It ensures compliance with health and safety regulations.

   C   It supports positive outcomes for children and families.

   D   It simplifies administrative tasks.

2 Which **one** of the following is the legislation in the United Kingdom that specifically promotes equality and diversity in childcare settings? (1 mark)

   A   Education Act 2002

   B   Childcare (Equality and Diversity) Act 2019

   C   Equality Act 2010

   D   Child Protection Act 2006

3 Why is it important to have positive and realistic expectations of children and young people? (1 mark)

   A   It follows the schools safeguarding policy. ☐

   B   It supports cognition and learning. ☐

   C   It discourages independence. ☐

   D   It improves academic outcomes. ☐

4 A new student from a minority ethnic background faces mockery from peers due to their cultural attire at secondary school.

   a   State the type of discrimination this student is facing. (1 mark)

   ....

   b   Describe **one** policy the school should have in place to prevent this type of discrimination. (2 marks)

   ....

   ....

   ....

   > **Tip**
   >
   > Consider which policies would need to be in place as preventative measures to support the staff and students.

5 Karina, a primary school teacher, notices one of her students, Aisha, an enthusiastic nine-year-old, has recently withdrawn from participating in group activities.

   a   Identify **one** possible barrier that could be affecting Aisha's participation in class. (1 mark)

   b   State **two** impacts this barrier may have on Aishas' wellbeing. (2 marks)

   c   Explain **two** strategies that the school could put in place to support Aisha. (6 marks)

   > **Sample answers**
   >
   > a   A barrier affecting Aisha could be socio-economic.
   > b   Aisha's family may have limited access to the extra resources to support her learning and this could affect her wellbeing.
   > c   One strategy is the school could provide computer and learning resources to help support Aisha, which could be linked to an individualised support plan for her. The plan could involve the teachers working with Aisha's parents and then having regular check-ins with a designated staff member to check on Aisha's anxiety. Another strategy could be starting a peer support programme for Aisha. The class teacher could pair Aisha with a supportive peer mentor to help her feel more comfortable during group activities. The peer support could offer encouragement and friendship to help her participate more. The family may need some financial guidance and support – the school can help with this even if it is directing them to the right place, for example Citizens Advice.

Chapter 10 Equality and Diversity

> **Analysis**
>
> The learner has made a fair attempt at answering each part of the question on barriers to participation. A good example has been given for Part a and would gain the 1 mark.
>
> The response for Part b is limited as it is not complete – 1 mark would be awarded here as only one impact has been included. Can you think of another impact on Aisha?
>
> Part c includes a very detailed response. It gives well explained strategies of how the school can support Aisha and her family to overcome any potential barriers. It is good to make positive connections with all families. This type of response would achieve the full 6 marks.

Now try answering the questions yourself.

a ....

....

b ....

....

....

....

c ....

....

....

....

....

....

....

....

....

6 Mya works as a classroom assistant at a primary school. She has been asked to review current legislation relating to equality and diversity.

Identify **two** of the protected characteristics as outlined in the Equality Act 2010 that ensure fairness and non-discrimination within the school environment. (2 marks)

....

....

....

....

Long-answer exam-style practice questions

1 Discuss the importance of promoting equality and diversity in early childhood settings.

Your response should demonstrate:

▷ how promoting equality and diversity can contribute to positive outcomes for children

▷ strategies that childcare providers should implement to create an inclusive environment

▷ the role that parents and caregivers play in supporting equality and diversity in early childhood settings.

(12 marks, plus 3 marks for QWC)

> **Plan your own answer**
>
> To answer this question thoroughly will require you to demonstrate your understanding of the principles of equality and diversity in the context of early childhood settings. You should also provide practical examples and strategies to support their points.
> Complete the table to help plan your answer for the first two bullet points.
>
> | Positive outcomes | Why? | Strategies to support an inclusive environment |
> |---|---|---|
> | Social and emotional development | Exposure to diverse environment helps children develop empathy and respect. | |
> | | | |
> | | | |
>
> Write some points here on the role of parents in supporting equality and diversity.
>
> ....
>
> ....
>
> ....
>
> ....

Chapter 10 Equality and Diversity

Using your notes from the planning space above, write your own response.

2 Nigel is a classroom assistant in a culturally diverse primary school. He observes a situation where one child is consistently excluded and mocked by their peers due to differences in their physical appearance. The child who is being targeted appears visibly upset and is starting to withdraw from social interactions.

Discuss how the school should address this situation in accordance with principles of equality, diversity and anti-discrimination practices within a primary school.

Your response should demonstrate:

▷ strategies for supporting the child who is being targeted

▷ approaches for educating the group of peers about diversity and inclusion

▷ the role of caregivers and parents in addressing and preventing such incidents.

(12 marks, plus 3 marks for QWC)

Hint

Include discussion on the impact that these strategies could have on addressing the issue.

3 Analyse how the celebration of cultural or religious festivals might impact the participation of children from diverse backgrounds in the school community.

Your response should demonstrate:

▷ understanding of the potential challenges or barriers that may arise for children from minority cultures or religions if their festivals are not acknowledged within the school environment

▷ strategies that schools can implement to ensure that these festivals are celebrated in a respectful, inclusive and sensitive manner while promoting active engagement among all students.

(12 marks, plus 3 marks for QWC)

Chapter 11 Special Educational Needs and Disability

Recall activities

1 Complete the following sentences.

   a The most important statutory guidance that sets out the duties, policies and procedures for all organisations in relation to special educational needs and/or disabilities (SEND) is:

   > **Hint**
   > Include the year with the name of the guidance.

   ....

   b This document supports children and young people between the ages of:

   ....

2 Complete the definitions for these acronyms and terms.

Acronym/Term	Meaning
SEND	
EHCP	
EHA	
Primary Disability	
Holistic	
Barrier to learning	

Chapter 11 Special Educational Needs and Disability

3. Identify **four** support assessments that are available in childcare for children with special educational needs before they are five years old. One has been added for you.

   1) 2 year progress check
   2) ....
   3) ....
   4) ....

4. Complete the table to list different ways speech can be supplemented or replaced by augmentative and alternative communication.

No-tech communication	Low-tech communication	High-tech communication
1)	1)	1)
2)	2)	2)
3)	3)	3)
4)	4)	4)

5. Complete the mind map to name policies and procedures that support children and young people with SEND. One policy has been listed for you.

> **Tip**
> Try to recall eight other policies.

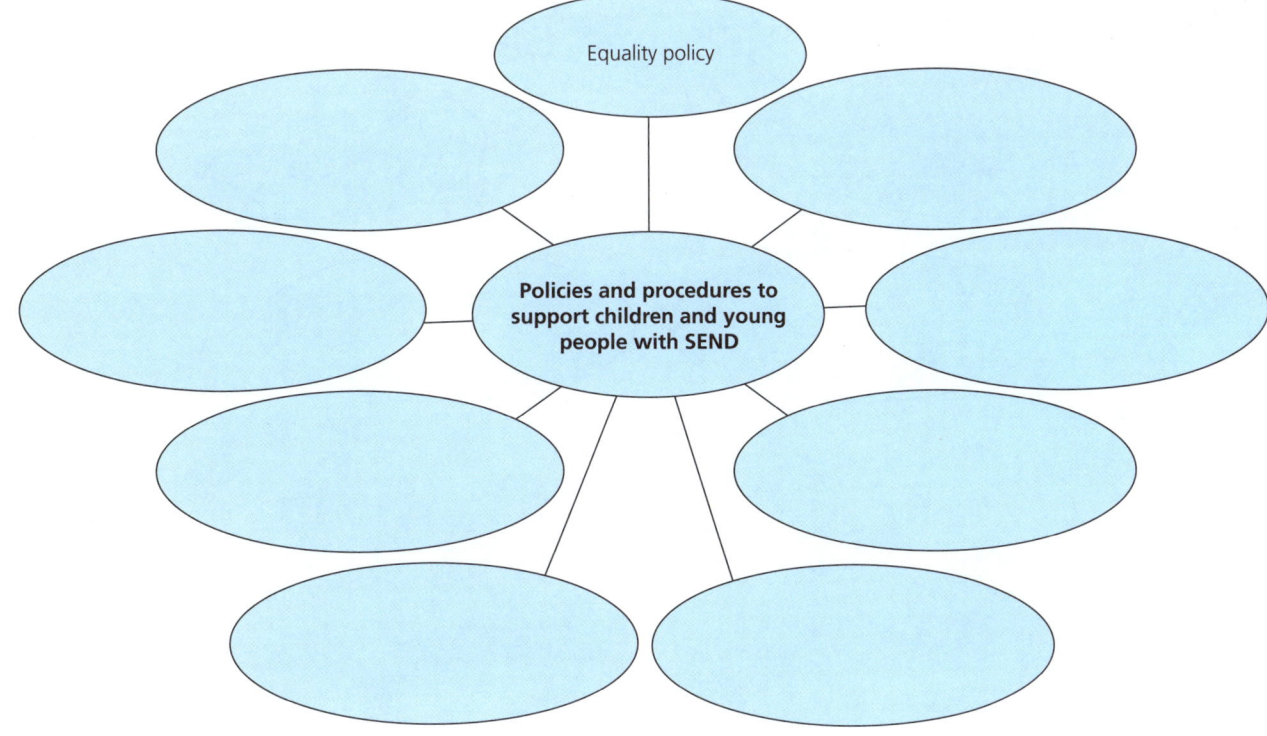

6 Cognitive difficulties may impact language, communication and educational development. List five impacts of cognitive difficulties on learning.

1) ....
....

2) ....
....

3) ....
....

4) ....
....

5) ....
....

7 a Complete the mind map below to identify **eight** chronic conditions. One has been added for you.

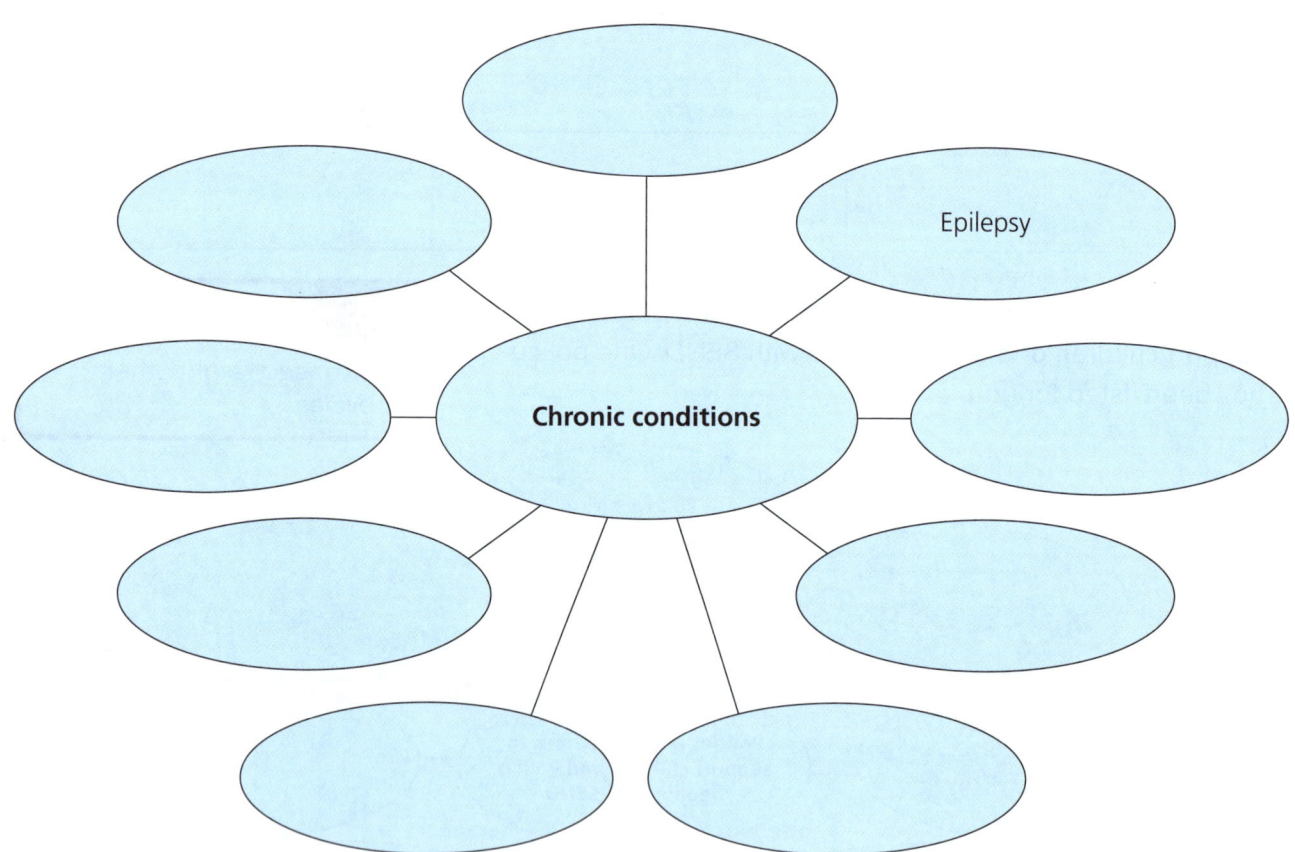

b Choose **four** of the conditions that you have identified in your mind map and add them to this table. In the second column identify how the condition might affect the child's emotions, education and quality of life. An example has been added to get you started.

Condition	Effects on the child
Epilepsy	This is a neurological condition that causes seizures that may be severe.

Short-answer exam-style practice questions

1 Which of **one** of the following is a policy that would be in place in a school to support children with SEND? (1 mark)

   A   homework policy

   B   uniform policy

   C   school admissions policy

   D   medical needs policy

2 Which **one** of the following is an example of low-tech communication? (1 mark)

   A   body language

   B   mobile devices

   C   picture exchange communication

   D   eye-tracking devices

3 Which **one** of the following is a cognitive difficulty? (1 mark)

   A   fine motor control

   B   language development

   C   mood and emotions

   D   logic and reasoning

4   Which **one** of the following correctly defines the term 'chronic health condition'? (1 mark)

    A   A condition that is long-standing, often lifelong. ☐

    B   A condition that is a physical disability. ☐

    C   A condition that requires one-to-one support. ☐

    D   A condition that is short-term. ☐

5   Education, health and care plans (EHCPs) are put in place to support children and young people with complex needs.

    a   Identify who can request an EHCP to be carried out. (1 mark)

    ....

    b   State the four steps of the graduated approach to providing SEN support. (1 mark)

        1) ....

        2) ....

        3) ....

        4) ....

6   A teacher observes a child with autism spectrum disorder (ASD) struggling to follow multi-step instructions and engage in structured activities. The child also has a visual impairment, further complicating their ability to process information.

    Describe **two** examples of how the combination of ASD and visual impairment impact the cvhild's cognitive skills in the childcare setting. (4 marks)

    > **Tip**
    > Consider the child's ability to navigate the environment.

    ....
    ....
    ....
    ....
    ....

7   Liam is seven years old and has type 1 diabetes. He is an energetic boy who loves to participate in various activities with his peers. However, managing his diabetes requires constant attention and care.

    > **Hint**
    > Remember, diabetes is a chronic health condition, that not only affects wellbeing but other aspects of development. Think about physical, psychological or social effects.

    a   Identify **two** ways that the diabetes may affect Liam. (2 marks)

    ....
    ....

Chapter 11 Special Educational Needs and Disability

b Describe how a teaching assistant could remove barriers and empower Liam in relation to his condition. (4 marks)

....

....

....

....

....

....

c Explain **two** reasons why the SENDCO needs to be in regular contact with Liam's parents. (6 marks)

> **Sample answer**
>
> c Having regular meetings will help the parents keep up to date with changes that are being in put in place at school for Liam. The school can then set up any support and resources for Liam.
>
> **Analysis**
> Good start to this question regarding keeping up to date with any changes. However, would benefit from further detail on the two reasons. Would it support building a positive relationship with his parents? What resources and support could be put in place? What about mentioning reviewing his individual Healthcare plan at the meeting? This response is likely to gain 2 marks.

Write your own answer to Part c here.

....

....

....

....

....

....

....

....

....

Long-answer exam-style practice questions

1 Mustafa, aged 11 years, has an EHCP. He attends a small village primary school and has a place at the secondary school in the nearest town.

Explain who the EHCP should be shared with and why this should happen.

Your response should demonstrate:

▷ knowledge of the purpose of an EHCP and its role in supporting Mustafa's needs

▷ understanding of the individuals and organisations involved in Mustafa's education and care

▷ reasoned judgements regarding how regular contact will help support a smooth transition to secondary school for Mustafa.

(12 marks, plus 3 marks for QWC)

Plan your own answer

Use the bullet points and the scenario to plan and structure your answer.

Start by adding some notes below on what an EHCP is and how it is going to help support Mustafa's needs.

....

....

....

....

Then identify the individuals who would be involved in Mustafa's education and care and why they are involved.

Individuals/organisations involved	Why?
Secondary School SENDCO	The SENDCO plays a crucial role in coordinating support for students with additional needs. Sharing Mustafa's EHCP will support a smooth transition for Mustafa from primary school to secondary school. It ensures a designated person will oversee the implementation of support strategies for Mustafa and address issues that may arise.

Chapter 11 Special Educational Needs and Disability

Individuals/organisations involved	Why?

Make some notes for how regular contact will help support a smooth transition to secondary school for Mustafa.

....
....
....
....

Now write your answer to this question.

....
....
....
....
....
....
....
....
....
....
....
....
....

Education and Early Years T Level Exam Practice Workbook

2 Anna works in a preschool. A child in her group, Jamie, is diagnosed as being on the autism spectrum. He struggles with social interactions and becomes overwhelmed in noisy environments.

Discuss how Anna could best support Jamie's inclusion and ensure his specific needs are met at preschool.

Your response should demonstrate:

▷ knowledge of the specific terminology that should be used when discussing Jamie's needs with other staff members, parents and external professionals

▷ understanding of the difference between integration, equity and inclusion in the context of supporting Jamie and other children with SEND in the preschool setting.

(12 marks, plus 3 marks for QWC)

> **Sample answer**
>
> It is important that Anna uses the right terminology and is respectful when she is discussing his needs to others. She should not say that Jamie is autistic but he is a child with autism. This is about him as an individual. It is important that Anna uses the correct language otherwise the other staff and jamies parents will become upset.
>
> Integration, equity and inclusion are the three principles that support children with SEND. Integration is about Jamie being included in the setting whereever possible and in all activities. Equity means that Jamie will get all the resources he needs at the setting tohelp him and is about making him feel like he belongs in the setting and is happy to be there.
>
> **Analysis**
>
> The learner has included good information in this response and has demonstrated understanding of integration, equity and inclusion. However, more detail could be added regarding ways Anna could support Jamie and the terminology Anna should use – what other language should she avoid? Why might Jamie's parents become upset with it? There are quite a few spelling mistakes and grammar errors that have affected the learner gaining further marks. It is important you read your work carefully to help gain the 3 extra marks for QWC. This response is likely to gain 7 marks out of 12 and 1 mark for QWC.

After reading the analysis of the sample answer, write your own answer here.

....
....
....
....
....
....
....

....
....
....
....
....
....

3 Mateo is a teaching assistant in a primary school. He has just started a new role supporting Jouri, a seven-year-old who has been diagnosed with an autistic spectrum disorder.

Explain what Mateo needs to consider when approaching this new role.

Your response should demonstrate:

▷ knowledge of the relevant policies that Mateo might need to refer to when starting this role

▷ the importance of using the correct terminology when discussing the needs of Jouri

▷ reasoned judgements regarding where Mateo could access the best support for this new responsibility.

(12 marks, plus 3 marks for QWC)

....
....
....
....
....
....
....
....
....
....
....
....
....
....

4 Nasreen attends a nursery school. She has recently been diagnosed with autism spectrum condition. Nasreen struggles with verbal communication and often becomes frustrated trying to express herself.

Discuss how practitioners in the nursery could support Nasreen's communication development using augmentative and alternative communication (AAC) methods.

Your response should demonstrate:

▷ understanding of the strategies that practitioners could implement to assess Nasreen's communication needs and preferences

▷ reasoned judgements regarding the benefits of AAC for children like Nasreen.

(12 marks, plus 3 marks for QWC)

Notes

2 Mia, a five-year-old girl, recently joined a Year 1 primary class. English is not her first language, and she is an English as an Additional Language (EAL) learner. Mia is adapting to a new culture, surroundings and educational system. Mia sometimes appears hesitant to participate in activities due to language barriers.

Discuss Mia's needs and how they can be supported in the school.

Your response should demonstrate:

▷ understanding of the need to collaborate effectively with Mia's parents to support her learning journey

▷ reasoned judgements on the importance of providing a language-rich environment for Mia and other EAL children in the school.

(12 marks, plus 3 marks for QWC)

> Write a list of strategies that practitioners can use to support Lucia and why they will help her, to plan your answer for the second and third bullet points.
>
> ....
> ....
> ....
> ....
> ....
> ....
> ....
> ....
> ....

Now write your answer, using your plan.

Chapter 12 English as an Additional Language

Long-answer exam-style practice questions

1. Lucia, aged four, has recently moved to the UK from Italy with her older sister Arianna, aged seven and her extended family. Lucia understands and speaks very little English.

   The staff in Lucia's reception class want to develop a range of strategies to support Lucia's acquisition of English as an additional language (EAL).

   Discuss how the setting can support Lucia and her family.

   Your response should demonstrate:

   ▷ knowledge of factors that could affect Lucia's acquisition of an additional language

   ▷ knowledge of a range of strategies that practitioners could embed to support Lucia

   ▷ reasoned judgements for why using those strategies will support Lucia and her family.

   (12 marks, plus 3 marks for QWC)

   > **Hint**
   >
   > For the last bullet point, you need to include **why** these strategies will help to engage Lucia and what impact they would have on her language acquisition. Remember the question is also asking for support for her family – do not forget to mention this in your answer.

Plan your own answer

Complete the table to structure your response to the first bullet point. Include three more factors.

Factors that could affect Lucia acquiring language	How could it affect Lucia
Transition from Italy	**Cultural shock** – understand and acknowledge the challenges Lucia may face adjusting to a new culture, environment and educational system. Lucia may be really missing her close friends and family in Italy – may be quieter than usual.

b Use **four** of the strategies from your mind map and complete the table by identifying how the strategy will support the children.

Strategy	How they can be used to support EAL children
Using drama and role play	Can build confidence – encourage conversations with others

Short-answer exam-style practice questions

1 Define the term 'receptive language'. (1 mark)

....

2 How long might Stage 3 of acquiring an additional language take? (1 mark)

    A 6 months–1 year ☐

    B 1–3 years ☐

    C 3–5 years ☐

    D 5–10 years ☐

3 State **two** of the five stages of acquiring an additional language. (2 marks)

   ....

   ....

4 Identify **two** professionals that may be available to provide schools with EAL children specific support and guidance. (2 marks)

   ....

   ....

5 It is important to have an inclusive approach to supporting EAL children in their development.

   a Identify which school policy having an inclusive approach would support. (1 mark)

   ....

   ....

   b Give **two** reasons why schools should celebrate a child's home language. (2 marks)

   ....

   ....

   ....

   ....

6 Darcus is an early years practitioner who works in a childcare centre where English is not the first language for many of the children. Ali recently joined the centre. Ali has limited English, having recently moved to the country with his family. Despite his language barrier Ali is eager to engage with his peers and participate in activities.

   Describe **two** ways that Darcus can support Ali acquiring a new language. (4 marks)

   > **Hint**
   >
   > Ali has shown that he likes interacting with his peers – consider what activities would engage him further in order to extend his language.

   ....

   ....

   ....

   ....

Chapter 12 English as an Additional Language

Recall activities

1 Complete the table by filling in the gaps on the five stages of acquiring language.

Stage	Characteristics
Silent/receptive	
	Begins to speak some words
Speech emergence	
	Increased use of spoken and written language

2 Write a list of factors that affect the acquisition of language. Two have been done for you.

> **Hint**
> Consider factors that could be personal to a child, family related or educational related factors. These could be examples from your own experience working with English as an Additional Language (EAL) children.

1) the learning environment

2) cultural background

3) ....

4) ....

5) ....

6) ....

7) ....

3 a Complete the mind map of the range of teaching strategies and resources that practitioners can use to support EAL children. One has been done for you.

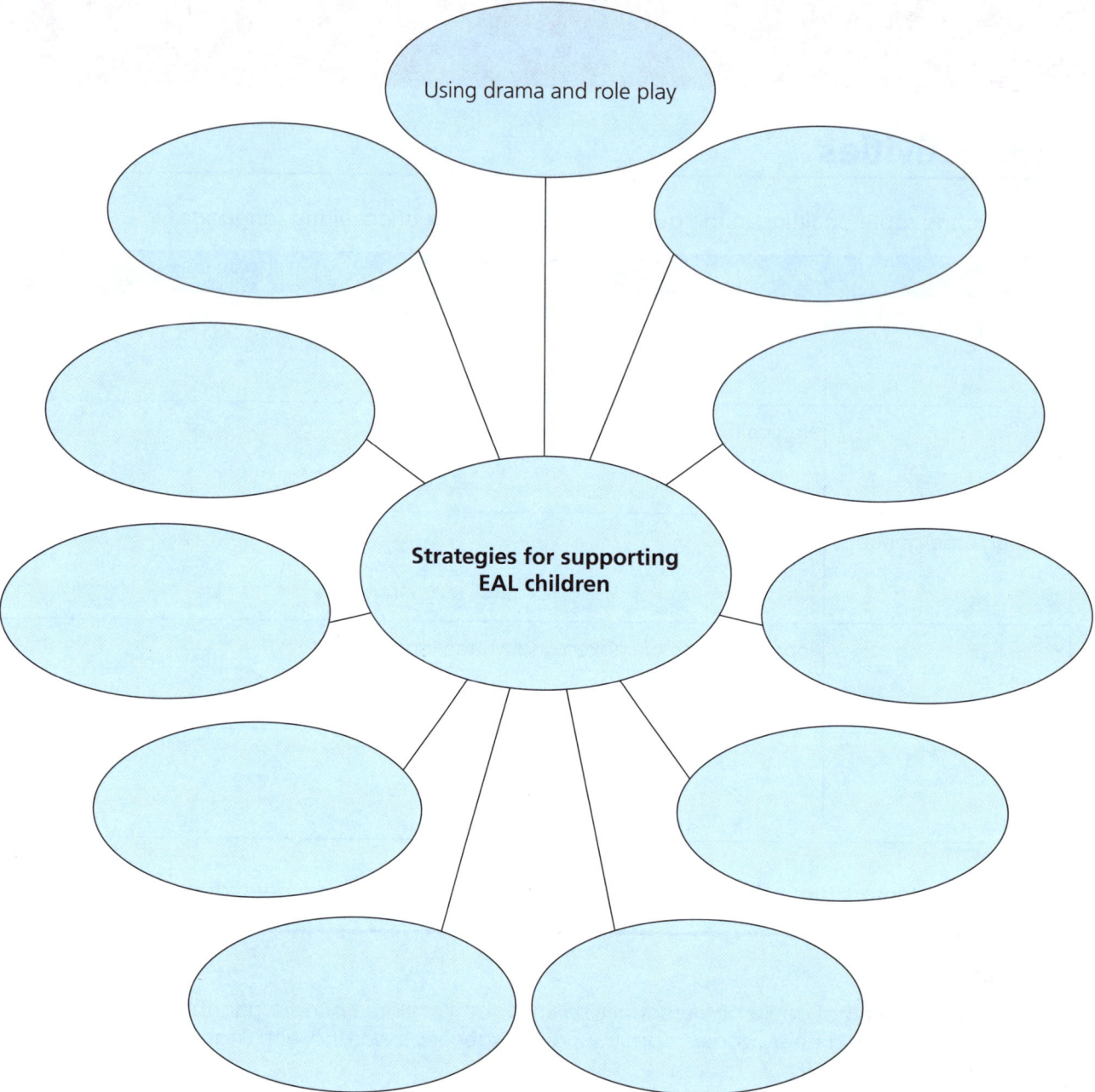

Notes

EDUCATION & EARLY YEARS: CORE
EXAM PRACTICE WORKBOOK

Develop the vital skills you need to achieve your best in the T Level exams with this accessible and engaging Exam Practice Workbook.

➡ Review and consolidate your knowledge, with varied recall activities for every topic including mind maps, fill in the blanks and more

➡ Reinforce your understanding and boost your exam confidence with both short- and long-answer exam-style practice questions, to help you break down the question

➡ Improve your exam technique with guidance on how to plan and review your responses, plus exam hints and sample student answers

Also available:

9781036005092 Education and Early Years T Level: Early Years Educator
9781036005108 My Revision Notes: Education and Early Years T Level

'T-LEVELS' is a registered trade mark of the Department for Education.

'T Level' is a registered trade mark of the Institute for Apprenticeships and Technical Education.

The T Level Technical Qualification is a qualification approved and managed by the Institute for Apprenticeships and Technical Education.

HODDER Education
+44 (0)1235 827827
education@hachette.co.uk
www.hoddereducation.com

ISBN 978-1-0360-0700-3